Solomon L.M. Conser

Virginia After the War

An account of three year's experience in reorganizing the Methodist Episcopal Church in Virginia at the close of the Civil War

Solomon L.M. Conser

Virginia After the War
An account of three year's experience in reorganizing the Methodist Episcopal Church in Virginia at the close of the Civil War

ISBN/EAN: 9783337403515

Printed in Europe, USA, Canada, Australia, Japan

Cover: Foto ©ninafisch / pixelio.de

More available books at **www.hansebooks.com**

Virginia After the War.

AN ACCOUNT OF THREE YEARS' EXPERIENCE IN REORGANIZING THE

METHODIST

EPISCOPAL CHURCH

IN VIRGINIA

———AT THE———

Close of the Civil War.

By REV. S. L. M. CONSER.

INDIANAPOLIS:
BAKER-RANDOLPH LITHO. & ENG. CO.,
1891.

Entered according to Act of Congress, July, 1891,

BY REV. S. L. M. CONSER,

In the office of the Librarian of Congress at Washington. D. C.

CONTENTS.

Chapter I . . . . To Virginia.
Chapter II . . . . Manassas.
Chapter III . . . . At Mr. M——'s House.
Chapter IV . . . . Wesley Chapel.
Chapter V . . . . The White Church.
Chapter VI . . . . Eccentric Genius.
Chapter VII . . . . Domestic Life.
Chapter VIII . . . . Discouraged.
Chapter IX . . . . Staunton.
Chapter X . . . . Emma.
Chapter XI . . . . Uphill Work.
Chapter XII . . . . "Tobe."
Chapter XIII . . . . Personal Devils.
Chapter XIV . . . . A Severe Test.
Chapter XV . . . . A Snake Story.
Chapter XVI . . . . Fairfax.
Chapter XVII . . . . "Born of Water."
Chapter XVIII . . . . Army Reminiscenses.

INTRODUCTION.

The following narrative was written at the repeated request of friends.

The events detailed occurred more than twenty years ago, and, as I kept no notes at the time, I have been obliged to write from memory. As some of the persons referred to are still living, I have thought it best to use fictitious initials.

I was born in Lewisburg, Pennsylvania, June 6, 1812. My father, John G. Conser—for many years a magistrate and an honored man in the community—was the only son of Henry Conser, one of the founders of Lewisburg. Henry Conser, my grandfather, was of Greek descent. But he and my father both died long before I could remember, and all I could learn of our Greek ancestor was that he lived somewhere along the Grecian archipelago, that he was captured by the English in a fight on the Mediterranean sea, and was taken to England, whence he migrated to this country early in the eighteenth century.

I was educated at Dickinson College, Carlisle, where I graduated in 1839. In 1840 I entered the Baltimore Conference, filling, during my itinerancy, appointments in Baltimore; also, a number of appointments in Pennsylvania and in Virginia.

The first two years of the Rebellion I served as chaplain of the Fifth Pennsylvania Reserve Corps. Afterwards I filled appointments at Duncannon and Gettysburg, then went to Virginia, where occurred the events recorded in the following pages.

At the close of my term in Virginia I retired from the

active ministry, having spent nearly thirty years in the service of my beloved Church.

I do not want to convey an impression that my life in Virginia was a series of hardships. On the contrary, I feel that God has always been good to me; and I have written this little book as an expression of gratitude, and with the hope that it may not only interest but spiritually benefit some of its readers.

S. L. M. Conser.

CHAPTER I.

TO VIRGINIA.

"Good morning, Bishop."

"This is Brother—'umph—I can not repeat your name, although I remember your remarks about lay delegation yesterday," replied the Bishop, with a pleasant smile, as he motioned me to a chair. It was the year 1866, and the Baltimore Conference, of which I was a member, was holding its annual session.

"Bro. Conser," I explained.

"Yes, yes; now I remember."

"Bishop," I continued, "I have not called on you to solicit a good appointment, as so many do, but rather to relieve you of one hard case. I have made up my mind to go to our Southern work."

"Why, Bro. Conser," replied the Bishop, somewhat surprised, "your appointment is already fixed, but I am really glad that you want to go South, as we are much in want of men for that field. Have you made any selection?"

"None at all, Bishop. I submit my appointment entirely into your hands."

"How would you like to go to Virginia?"

"Bishop, I would like to go to the hottest place in the South. I am not afraid; I helped to whip them, and now I want to help to raise them up."

"Bro. Conser, you will find it hot enough in Virginia, but I will transfer you to Bishop Scott, who has charge of that work."

And so I reported to Bishop Scott, who referred me to Rev. E. P. Phelps as my Presiding Elder. I was intimately acquainted with E. P. Phelps. We met in Baltimore and arranged that I should go to Southern Virginia, make my headquarters somewhere along the James river, and reorganize as best I could the old Methodist Episcopal Church.

After locating my family in Baltimore, I started for my hazardous field of labor. The first night of my journey I spent in Washington, or, rather, what was left of Washington City at the close of the war. Before the war Washington was little better than a scattered group of villages, almost swamped in mud in winter and smothered in dust in summer. During the war many of its inhabitants had gone South, where their sympathies were, and many houses had been abandoned to the chances of war; the remaining population seemed surly, and I was glad to get away from the place. I had camped at Tenallytown, or Georgetown Heights, and Arlington, from August, 1861, to March, 1862, during which time I was much in the city, and had seen all that was worth seeing in the shabby capital of the United States; so I cared not to spend any time there on this occasion. As soon as the train was ready we moved towards Alexandria, on the Virginia side of the Potomac. In looking upon that river I was reminded of a ludicrous incident that occurred while we were encamped at Arlington in 1862. I had occasion to go to Washington one day, and in order to get through the guards at the chain bridge I must use the pass-word. The pass-word that day was "Potomac." When I reached the bridge the guard demanded the countersign. I very politely whispered in his ear "Potomac;" and was about to hasten on. "No, sir, no!" was the gruff reply of the Irish sentinel, and his grim-looking musket caused me to halt.

"Where is your corporal?" I inquired. "Will you call for him?"

"Certainly," he replied, and soon the military official put in an appearance.

"What is wrong?" inquired the sergeant.

"This fellow," said Pat, "hasn't the pass-word."

"Yes I have," said I.

The sergeant called me aside and inquired who I was, and the countersign, and after hearing my reply, he remarked, "All right!"

He then stepped up to the guard and said, "What is the countersign?" On hearing Pat's reply, he exclaimed, "Buttermilk! Who in the name of heaven gave you that for a pass-word?" Pat answered that Fritz Crumacher, his predecessor, had so informed him. Fritz was at once summoned, and when he was asked for the countersign, responded in his Teutonic style, "Pot—o—mac," accenting the first part of the word broadly; the mystery was solved. Nobody was wrong but Pat, and I passed peacefully on my way.

And now we are in Alexandria. This city is situated on a beautiful plateau on the west bank of the Potomac river. It is regularly laid out; its wide streets running east, west, north and south. Its buildings are antique, and its citizens conservative. Originally, it was in the District of Columbia, but now it is the capital of Alexandria county, Virginia. It is a dilapidated town—no manufactories, no commerce, no enterprise. How the 8,000 or 10,000 inhabitants manage to live is a mystery. The country round about is in keeping with the town. Denuded of its original forests, it presents a most forlorn and desolate appearance.

The only life in the picture is a farmer in "butternut" coat and broad-brimmed hat, with long hair and a frizzly red beard, who "totes" along the road to town with a load of wood amounting to, possibly, a quarter of a cord, mounted on a rickety vehicle drawn by a steer. The proceeds of this cargo may reach $1.37½, with which wealth the yeoman purchases some coffee, sugar, nails, etc. Then, after exhausting his cash in paying for his last drink, he starts home with an empty pocket but a contented mind.

The next week witnesses the same routine, and so month after month, and year after year. Many of the inhabitants of this part of Virginia live about as happily, and much in the condition of their four-footed neighbors of the woods. Paul's admonition to Timothy is practically observed here, "Having bread and raiment let us be content."

Chickens and turkeys thrive and grow fat on grasshoppers and tobacco worms.

CHAPTER II.

MANASSAS.

At Alexandria I took the Orange Railroad for Manassas —famous for the disastrous battle of Bull Run. Bull Run is a small stream conducting the waste water of this sterile country along its sleepy way to the Potomac. The vegetation, although sparse and scanty in this section, was sufficient to mercifully hide all traces of the dreadful battle. But the Northern men on the train were anxious to see Manassas. "Where is Manassas, Uncle?" inquired one of a grizzly old negro, when the train halted. "Lor, Massy, you're in Massus now," he replied. We looked around and saw a tavern, a small store and a blacksmith shop! And this was Manassas.

"Anything to drink here, landlord?" said another, stepping up on the platform.

"Plenty, plenty," was the answer.

"Well, let's have a glass of wine."

"Have no wine, sir."

"Well, what have you to drink; whisky, brandy?"

"No, sir. Have plenty of apple-jack."

"Well, that's all you do have, I suppose. Let's have some," demanded the thirsty traveler.

The decanter is brought out and all are invited to partake, but no one appears to relish the precious beverage. The dime is tossed on the counter, the conductor shouts

"All aboard!" and away we roll through a dismal country toward Gordonsville. The army-worm had left its trail over the impoverished country. The people, if ever there had been any, had left it. But few shanties and still fewer houses could be seen, and these were for the most part occupied by ex-slaves, and were rudely furnished with superannuated camp utensils. Dogs and chickens were occasionally seen, but no cattle. All fences were gone and all landmarks eliminated. How a whip-poor-will could live in that country was a mystery. A few buzzards soared around, subsisting on the remains of defunct army horses.

A serious question arose in my mind: "*Was such a forlorn country worth fighting for?*"

From Gordonsville—a town of about two hundred inhabitants—we continued our journey to Charlottesville. The country here assumes a different and improved aspect. White people make their appearance, and agriculture receives some attention. Incipient or diminutive mountains begin to appear, and beautiful field flowers are abundant. Few men not railroad employes, and still fewer women, are to be seen, and those who were visible appeared surly and sad. The virus of treason and the mortification of military defeat had cast a wet blanket of sorrow and sadness over all. The country looked not unlike a desolated country graveyard, and the people not unlike the sad spectres flitting among the tombs. I almost thought I could realize the solemn emotions of the immortal Watts when he indited his famous funeral dirge, "Hark! from the tombs a doleful sound."

But such are the results of war. I could think only of Julius Cæsar's comment, when, looking on his slain countrymen, he sadly remarked, "They would have it so."

The cup of sorrow this people mixed for others was put to their own lips.

Charlottesville is quite a flourishing town—the capital of Albemarle county. This place approaches the mountains and is somewhat removed from the plains of Tuckahos. There is something in mountain air that inspires a thirst for freedom. The Highlanders of Scotland and the Albigenses of France, long resisted the thralldom of royalty, as did the mountaineers of West Virginia, Kentucky and Tennessee the folly of secession. It was in the uplands and mountains of the South that first was sung with good will,

"The Star Spangled Banner, long may it wave,
O'er the Land of the Free, and the Home of the Brave."

But away we go, over the valleys and mountains to Staunton, in Augusta county, Virginia. Staunton, a well built town, is located in the famous Cumberland valley, the most productive, and the wealthiest section on the Atlantic coast.

In Staunton I met my Presiding Elder, who had, with great difficulty—so bitter was the feeling towards all Northern people—procured a home for the use of his family. Though a Virginian by birth and education, yet simply because of his loyalty, he was shunned as a Syrian leper, and his family might as well have lived in the desert of Sahara as on the principal street of the town, as far as any social recognition was concerned.

The house he had succeeded in renting had only four rooms, with the kitchen in the cellar.

In Staunton, also, though nature bloomed, nature's children mourned. The dark pall of treason cast dark shadows all around. Alas! the "lost cause!!" Alas! Alas!! Treason's dark flag was furled, nor dare to flaunt its venom where the stars and stripes triumphantly floated; and well might the deluded dupes sing

"The warrior's flag departs, to meet the warrior's soul."

But I could not stay long in Staunton. My charge was to be Jackson River Station. I was told to make my way to the home of Bro. G——, who was a loyal man and a true Methodist. Said Phelps—" Bro. G—— will give you valuable information in reference to your work, and when you get into trouble let me know. Meantime I will keep Secretary Stanton advised as to our treatment by the 'secesh.' Good-bye!" and with these re-assuring words he left me.

I jumped aboard the train and away we sped. The railroad made some strange and, to my thought, very unnecessary turns; but I was informed that the road was thus located to please one of the stockholders, and of course the explanation was satisfactory.

CHAPTER III.

AT MR. M——'S HOME.

When Jackson River Station was reached I left the train to continue my journey on foot. It was night. Where should I go? Years before, in the early days of my itinerancy, I had traveled through this same section of country, and I tried now to bring to mind the names and residences of my friends of former days. It was quite possible that some of them might still be living in this vicinity. I thought of Mr. M——, whose home, as I recollected, used to be near this place. A colored uncle happened to pass just at this moment and I hailed him. "Uncle, where does Mr. M—— live?" Somewhat to my surprise, but greatly to my joy, he replied that he lived "jus' up dar." "Up where?"

"Dat his place jus' dar. Jus' gwang up de trac' an' tote to de right dar," he answered.

Up the track I "toted" in the fast-increasing darkness. But I missed my way, got entangled in the bushes, then retraced my steps to the railroad track, fell into a cow-trap, crawled out and scraped off the mud, heard the dogs bark, and following the sound reached a house. I rapped, the door opened, and I inquired for Mr. M——. I was requested to walk in, and I gladly obeyed.

"And who are *you*?" inquired Mr. M——. "No matter who I am, I want my supper and a bed to sleep in. Betty, is my room ready?" I added, turning towards the girl who had admitted me.

"I'm not Betty," answered the astonished maid.

"Well, you used to be," I retorted.

"Did you know Betty? Why, Betty done dead long ago," said Mr. M——, eyeing me curiously.

"Where is George?" I continued, not appearing to notice his growing curiosity.

"George lives in Kansas," he replied, drawing nearer to me, "and was in the Yankee army and *fought for the North*." This last in a tone implying he could scarcely impart news that would show George up in a more dreadful light. *Fought for the North!*

"Pap," said I, familiarly, putting down my carpet-bag and helping myself to a chair, "I think you are mistaken. I was in what you rebels called the Yankee army, and I ought to know something about it. We did *not* fight for the *North;* we fought for the *Union.* You "rebs" wanted to go out of the Union, and we "Yanks" fought to keep you in, and we whipped you, too."

"Are you a 'Yank'?" he asked, astonished at my bold words.

"I suppose that is what you would call me," I quietly replied, at the same time taking a covert look around to see what indications there were of supper.

"Well, are you ashamed of it?" said he, on hearing my admission of guilt.

"No sir, no!" I retorted. "I am not. My old friend, do you really think that I could ever be ashamed of the country my grandfather helped to make in the revolution?"

"Why, was your grandfather in the revolution," he exclaimed, edging his chair around so as to get a better view of my face.

"My grandfather was a soldier in the Revolutionary War, and was fatally wounded in the battle of Brandywine. My father was a lieutenant in the war of 1812 when I was born, and I was a chaplain in the late war," I replied with some pride at the military record of my family.

"Who in thunder are you any-way?" he blurted out.

"Never mind. I want my supper," said I, as a feeling of "goneness" began once more to assert itself.

Just then the tea-bell sounded.

"There," said he, "supper is ready now. Come out and have some." And I gladly followed him to the table.

"Mr. M——," I said when we were seated, will you allow me to say "grace" before we eat?"

"Why, yes. But I would like to know who you are."

"Well, I'm no rebel, that's certain. Another thing equally certain, I'm hungry."

"Say prayers," was his answer.

And then with serious earnestness I prayed. "Great God look kindly upon this family and bless them! Bring them penitently back to the country from which they have strayed, and the Church from which they have wandered. Bless us all and save us all, for Christ's sake. Amen!"

"I wonder you are not afraid to talk so and pray that way in this country," said Mr. M.——, after a brief pause during which he piled my plate with the plain food spread before us.

"When I am in the right I am afraid of no man," I answered quietly.

"In the right! Don't you think *we* were in the right, too?"

"No, sir; no! You were all wrong, and all the time wrong."

"And so were you," he retorted.

2

"No, no. We were right, all right, and all the time right, and you know it," was my rejoinder, as I passed up my cup to be refilled.

"You're no Yankee," he exclaimed, "or Yankees are not all alike. There's a Yankee down at the saw-mill and he doesn't talk like you do. But please tell us your name."

"Pap, I think I know his name," spoke up one of the children. "Ain't you Mr. Phelps?" turning towards me.

"What, E. P. Phelps?" I asked.

"I mean the old Presiding Elder. He has turned to be a great Yankee," answered the girl.

"Why, he's a native born Virginian," I remarked.

"Well, but he went with the North," she persisted.

"When you say he 'went with the North' I suppose you mean he remained loyal to the Church and State," I replied.

"*You* would call it so," was the answer.

"And that is the right way to call it," I continued. "Hence we loyal folks call you 'rebs,' 'traitors.'"

"Oh, do not use that word, it is so offensive," spoke up Mr. M——.

"And whose fault is it? You were once a 'Squire. Please define treason."

"Oh, I know what the Constitution says, but please do not accuse *us* of treason," he returned, moving uneasily in his chair.

"Then please do not be guilty of it."

"But do tell us what is your name," said Mr. M., as we arose from the table and walked into the sitting-room.

"Whether I tell you my name or not, I can easily tell you what I am, I'm sleepy," I returned, hiding a great yawn.

"Tommy," turning to one of his boys, "show this

stranger to his room. Good-night," and he went out abruptly without forcing me to reveal my identity.

When I came down in the morning at the call of the breakfast bell I said, "Mr. M——, may we have family prayers before breakfast?"

"Not unless you tell us your name," he answered with a determined air. "You talk so much like a young preacher who used to stop here many years ago by the name of 'Conser,' but I believe he is dead."

"Did you know Conser?" I queried with some interest. "He was a singular genius."

"Yes, but he was honest," replied Mr. M——, with fervor.

"While he preached here I sold a gal, and he said I did wrong, and I was ashamed of myself, and I regretted it and have ever since. I know slavery was wrong."

"I think that man Conser is still living," I remarked.

"I'll bet if he's still living that he is no 'secesh,'" he returned promptly.

"I think he was in the Union army," I said.

"Why, did Methodist preachers go in the army?"

"He, I think, went as a chaplain," I replied.

"Was he killed?"

"He was wounded and very sick, but I believe he escaped with his life."

"Is he still preaching?" he asked without any apparent suspicion of my identity. "Oh but I would like to see him, he was quite a favorite with mother. She always called him 'honest Conser,' and my son was converted under his preaching."

"Was he opposed to slavery?" I asked.

"Oh, yes; that was all the people had against him."

"I suppose he was too honest for the people," I suggested.

"Yes, on that *pint* he was, but still they liked him. Do you know him?" he added looking more closely at me.

"Oh yes, I have known him for years. We Methodist preachers all know each other."

"Did you say he was still living?"

"I do say so."

"Well, do you know where he is?" a suspicion of the truth beginning to dawn upon his mind. "Yes," I said smiling and extending my hand, "he is now talking to his old friend." A hearty shake followed. We chatted pleasantly during our morning meal, of old times and old friends, and then bidding my host good-by and thanking him for his hospitality to a "stranger," I began what proved to be a long and dreary walk in search of another old friend, Bro. Circle.

The Jackson river meanders through the Alleghany mountains and enters the James at Buchanan. It is a dreary section of country, with roads that reminded me of the closing lines of that stanza written by Watts:

> "Broad is the road that leads to death,
> And many walk together there;
> But wisdom shows a narrow path,
> With here and there a traveler."

At length I reached Bro. Circle's place. The house looked just as of yore, with its vine-covered piazza and front yard full of flowering shrubs—cape jessamines—I think they call them. I noticed the old lady standing in the doorway. I approached and saluting her, inquired, "Can an old Methodist preacher find entertainment here to-night?"

"I dunno. Go in an' ask the old man," she replied indifferently. I entered.

"This is Bro. Circle, I believe."

"Yes, yes; but who are you?" he inquired, with some surprise.

"I? Why I am an old Methodist preacher."

"Which side do you belong to?" he demanded.

"Bro. Circle, I belong to the *right* side, as I always did.'

Almost instinctively he replied, "You belong to the *old* side," conscious that the *old* side was the *right* side. "But," he continued, "we have all left the old Church."

"And you did very wrong, and your children may find it so when you are dead."

"What is your name?" he inquired.

"My name is Conser."

"What! the Conser that used to preach on this Circuit?"

"Yes, sir; I am that very Conser."

"Why, why, Bro. Conser, is it possible?" And he shook my hand long and earnestly.

"Bro. Circle," I finally said, "can I find entertainment here to-night? I can pay for my accommodations."

"Bro. Conser, you sit down. You're not going away to-night;" and he called to the old lady to come and see an old friend.

A good supper of "johnny cake," sausage and milk revived my weary frame, and we returned to the sitting-room to chat a little longer.

"But what are you going to do down here?" Bro. C—— inquired.

"I am going to try to reorganize the old Methodist Episcopal Church in this country."

"But we're all going to the Church South," he returned.

"So much the worse for you, and now is your time to come back."

"How can we while that new chapter is in your discipline?"

"What new chapter?"

"Why, the chapter that frees all our slaves."

"There is no such chapter in the discipline," I replied in astonishment.

"Oh! yes, there is."

"Did you ever see it?"

"No; but I heard one preacher talk of it."

"Did you ever hear your preacher *read* it?"

"No; but I heard them talk of it often."

"So you never read it, nor heard it read? I would advise you to read it for yourself, and then you will know the real truth of the matter. But enough of this. I want to know about your children and the folks in the neighborhood. What has become of Stephe?"

"Stephe? Oh! he lives in West Virginia. And, Bro. Conser, what do you think? Stephe is a *black* Republican! But he is rich," he added by way of apology, or in extenuation of Stephe's disreputable political condition.

"Is he still religious?" I asked.

"Yes; he seems to be, and he still holds on to the old Church."

"Good for Stephe!" I said. "I only wish you all had done as he did. Are any of the B——'s living yet?" I added.

"Well, yes. You remember Walter? Well, he went into the army, and, they say, deserted. His mother went crazy, and the old man killed himself, and all the family are scattered 'round. A Yankee has got the old place, and cheated the heirs out of their share of the money."

And so we chatted on of old times and friends and of the great changes the terrible war had wrought, until it was time to retire for the night. In the morning, as I was taking leave, I offered to pay my host for his kindness in my entertainment, but he would not listen to such a proposition. I thanked him, and then waited for his parting instructions.

"Go right down the road there to Mr. R——'s and tell him you want dinner, and to charge it to me. He is a 'secesh,' and be careful you don't quarrel."

And so I trudged along down the road, such as it was, until I arrived at Mr. R——'s, where I received a good dinner without any difficulty and without indulging in any unnecessary flow of language. The "secesh," learning of my destination, kindly furnished me with a horse and a mounted escort in the person of his son. In such fine and comfortable style I pursued my journey several miles, until we reached my objective point—the home of Bro. G——. Here I met with sincere friends, and eventually made this home my headquarters.

CHAPTER IV.

WESLEY CHAPEL.

Brother G—— owned a mill and a store and an immense tract of land, and he exerted considerable influence in the community in which he lived. A man's influence in Virginia is measured more by the length of his purse than by his worth. In Mr. G——'s case, however, both these requisites were happily united.

"I suppose you will preach for us on Sunday," said my friends after they had offered me bodily refreshments and learned from me the object of my coming.

"Well, yes," I replied, "if there will be a congregation to preach to."

"You shall have a congregation. We have a class in the morning, so you had better preach in the evening, at three o'clock."

I agreed, and on going to the church at the time appointed, found it full. We had a good service and at the close I announced preaching for next Sunday at ten o'clock A. M. With the next Sunday came crowds, some to hear, others merely to see the "Yankee Preacher," and I was requested to make an appointment for Piny Grove, several miles to the south. Soon after this I was waited upon by Dr. J——, who inquired whether I had authorized an appointment to preach at Piny Grove. I said I had.

"Well, Mr. Conser," continued the Doctor, "I am authorized by the people of that neighborhood to request you not to come. We held a meeting and concluded now that the war was over, that your preaching would only stir up strife and might make trouble, and as they had a preacher of their own at Piny Grove, it would be better for the peace of the community if you did not come."

"Please tell your constituents," I returned with some asperity, "that the 'Yankee Preacher' knows his own business and will attend to it."

"And you intend to come?"

"In the name of the Lord, and under the protection of my country's flag I expect to."

"Well, I'm afraid it will make trouble."

"All right, *I'll* make no trouble. I'm a loyal and law-abiding citizen of the U. S., and the U. S. can, and will protect me. I'll attend to my duty as directed by my Church."

"What Church do you represent?" he asked.

"I am sent here to organize the M. E. Church."

"You mean the Church North," he interposed.

"No, sir, I do not. I mean just what I say, the Methodist Episcopal Church."

"But, Mr. Conser, you know that in 1844 the M. E. Church was divided into the Church North, and the Church South?"

"No, Doctor, I know no such thing. I know that a parcel of slave-holders and slavery advocates seceded and organized a bogus church of their own, and called it the M. E. Church South," I replied, emphasizing my words.

"Well," said he, seeing it was useless to attempt to change my purpose, "I suppose you are the right man to stir up strife?"

"No more than my Savior was. Tell your friends, that

all being well, I will be at Piny Grove at the time appointed. Good evening."

The Doctor having failed with me, went to my host Mr. G—— and tried to prevail upon him to use his influence to prevent my keeping my appointment; but I was firm. I knew that to yield an inch at the commencement of my labors was equivalent to yielding all, and I determined to conquer or die in the attempt. I would allow no traitor to dictate to me. The next I heard was that a company of sixty or more of the so-called "Southern Chivalry" had formed themselves into a company to duck me in the river if I attempted to preach at Piny Grove. Oh, for shame! A company of sixty to duck one poor little Yankee preacher! During the week I received a note from Capt. L——, near Piny Grove, requesting me to call and see him. I promptly replied to the note in person. Capt. L——, who was an ex-Confederate, was fortunately at home.

"Are you the Yankee preacher?" he demanded, looking hard at me.

"That is what some call me."

"Are you going to preach in our church?"

"What is your church?" I inquired in return.

"I mean Piny Grove."

"I have an appointment there on Sunday a week, captain."

"Do you intend to fill it?"

"I do."

"Do you know that you will get a ducking if you do?" he continued.

"I heard that such an attempt would be made," I quietly returned.

"Ain't you afraid?"

"Not much. Ducking means to be immersed in water,

and I have been immersed many a time," I replied with a faint smile.

"Were you in the 'Yankee' army?" he said after a pause.

"I was a chaplain in the Union army."

"Were you wounded?"

"I was, but not seriously," I replied.

"How came a chaplain to be wounded?" he asked incredulously. "I thought chaplains were never about only on pay days."

"Captain, I was in the seige of Richmond, and during the seven days' fight I volunteered to carry wounded soldiers from the front, and I was so engaged when a sliver of a shell struck me."

"Did you go to the hospital for this wound?" he inquired with considerable interest.

"No, sir. I afterward went to the hospital for camp fever."

"Did you ever see any Confederates?"

"Thousands and thousands of them."

"Did you ever try to relieve any of them?"

"I did when not otherwise engaged," I replied.

"I have heard something of your war history, and from what I have heard and what I see, you are not a coward, but I think you should have been a captain, and not a chaplain. But do you really intend to preach at Piny Grove?"

"Certainly, I do."

"Bravo! Chaplain, give me your hand. There is a company in this neighborhood that has threatened to duck you, but I have a company, too; and if the others attempt to hurt you, depend upon it there will a be lively ducking that day."

"Captain, how many have they in their company?"

"They say sixty-five."

"How many have you, captain?"

"I have thirty-four."

"Captain," said I, "I do not wish you to get into trouble on my account. Dr. J—— told me that my enemies were desperate fellows."

"Dr. J—— is one of them," he exclaimed; "and I'll make the whole party skedaddle with a dozen of my men. Just you come on."

When the eventful day and hour arrived, six or eight of my friends from Wesley Chapel (brave fellows), accompanied me on horseback to Piny Grove. Somehow I had given up the idea of being ducked, and thought I would be shot. This could easily have been done in a crowd without the detection of the murderer, and my impression was that they would watch until I was entering the church and that then I would fall mortally wounded.

As we approached the church, my escort, one after the other, gradually fell back until I was left alone. There was a dense crowd around the church. I hitched my horse. My heart was beating with terrific throbs, but outwardly I gave no sign of the commotion within. As I approached, the crowd parted, as if by common consent, and I was scrutinized by hundreds of inquisitive eyes. I advanced to the door of the church. As I drew near the door the crowd closed behind me. My heart began to fail me. "Shall I retreat," I thought. "Life is sweet. Must I sacrifice it simply to attest my bravery? Will God stand by me in this emergency?" And then came another thought, "I risked my life for my country, and do I care less for my church? God help me; here goes." One, two, three steps, and I was within the threshold, and they began to sing—the church was crowded—"Come thou fount of every blessing." I thought I could leap to the ceiling. God has saved me! was my inward cry of gratitude. Near the door stood my friend Capt. L——. I entered the pulpit and went through with the service. During the progress of the meeting some old sisters, forgetful of present surroundings commenced shouting, one exclaiming, no doubt to the annoyance of many around her, "Glory to God! The good old times are coming back." At the close of the service I announced another appointment at an early date, and shaking hands with my new friend, Capt. L——, I departed in company with as many of my brave escort as I could readily find. The ducking party of sixty-five had not put in an appearance.

This adventure at Piny Grove had much to do with my subsequent success in that section; for though I met with the most determined opposition, clandestinely, no more citizen committees waited upon me to impede my progress. At this critical time I was much indebted to not a few members of the M. E. Church South for helping to compose my congregations at various times at Piny Grove, and I often found friends in unexpected quarters.

CHAPTER V.

THE WHITE CHURCH.

Shortly after the events just recorded, I was invited to preach at the White Church. On Saturday night I went to the home of Bro. S——, one of the members, and was kindly entertained. On Sunday morning we set out for the church, which was several miles away. After we had gone a short distance, Bro. S—— remarked that he was obliged to call upon a sick neighbor, and, promising to follow me shortly, he left me to pursue my way alone. When I reached the church I found it locked. But a large crowd had gathered outside. I knew no one, and no one appeared to know me, but I soon discovered that I had a crowd of enemies to address. There had been a picnic or Sunday-school celebration in a neighboring grove and the seats were still there. I immediately went into the grove and began to sing. The crowd gathered around me. I preached as best I could, and all was as quiet as a mouse in the pantry or burglars in a bank. At the close of the sermon I said I had something more to say after the benediction. All remained, and I said in substance: "Friends, although a stranger to you, I am not altogether a stranger to this country. My name is S. L. M. Conser, a member of the Baltimore Conference of the Methodist Episcopal Church—not the Methodist Episcopal Church North, not the Methodist Episcopal Church South; I disdain to belong to a sectional church. I am, I believe, the only representative, in this section, of the most numerous, the most wealthy and the most pious church on the American continent. As to my business, I am here by the authority of my God and my church. God has called me to preach, and Bishop Scott has sent me here to preach, and I am going to do it. You may kill me—and some of you would only be too glad to do it, did not the shadow of the gallows loom up before you—but that does not scare me; you would gain nothing in the end. Now, if your courts or criminal officers have any business with me, here I am, ready to go to jail, and I will look to the country I helped to save for my protection; but I am not here to be a foot-ball for fools, depend upon it!" Instead of groaning they cheered me. I continued: "Now, all being well, in four weeks I will be here again." A man stepped from the crowd and said, "Conser, the next time you come this way stop with me." In four weeks I returned to the White Church appointment. My new friend who had offered me entertainment was *away from home*, but his son treated me kindly. On Sunday morning, when I went to the stable for my horse, he had disappeared. We looked around carefully, but no horse was to be seen. Sad as I felt, I tried to conceal my grief, and we went to the house for breakfast. While sitting at the table a colored boy came along and asked, "Mas'r N——, whose horse is dat in de rail pen?" "Where do you mean, Ike?" "Jus' up dar, Mas'r." So we went with "Ike," and, sure enough, up the road a short distance stood my horse, snugly confined in a pen of rails barely large enough for him to stand erect in. The horse was uninjured, but very hungry. I did not gratify the miscreants who played this practical joke by ever referring to it in public. My strange friend who so cordially invited me at my first visit had evidently been carried beyond the bounds of discretion by his emotional impulses, but when he saw or learned the prevailing sentiment of his neighbors, he regretted his offer of hospitality and made it *convenient* to leave home when I was expected. Of all slaves to public opinion the Virginian is the most abject. In the same place where I was so loudly applauded at my first visit, I was subsequently hung in effigy! Some brainless simpletons constructed a hideous effigy, labeled it "The Last of the Yanketee Pritcher," and suspended it from a limb of an oak tree in front of the White Church. How gladly they would have hung the "Yanketee Pritcher" without the effigy had they not been afraid.

While in that neighborhood I called on Capt. L——, who so bravely proctected me before. He received me with much apparent kindness. Referring to my first visit to Piny Grove, he inquired whether I knew what had become of my ducking party. I said:

"No, I have been away ever since. Have you heard anything?"

"Yes, I heard all about it. On Saturday, a week before you were to preach here, they had a mustering, and when the name Conser Purcell was called, Joe Aspen who stood next, said: 'Purcell, where did you get that name "Conser" from?'

"'Why,' answered Purcell, 'when I was born there was a Methodist preacher on this circuit by that name and he baptized me, and my mother liked him so much that she gave me his name.'

"'Why, that is the Yankee preacher's name.'

"'*It is'nt!*' exclaimed Purcell. 'Well they say so!' answered Joe. Presently another name attracted attention. 'John Conser Wolf.' A few words of inquiry brought out the fact that 'John Conser Wolf' was also a namesake of the Methodist preacher who had traveled that circuit years ago, and a little further investigation led to the conclusion that the 'Yankee Preacher' and the 'Methodist Conser' were one and the same.

"'Well if that is so, I won't help duck him,' exclaimed Wolf. 'Why he baptized me.' 'Nor will I,' said Purcell. 'Why mother thinks he is an angel.'"

"Then the captain stepped forward and said: 'Boys this ends the ducking fun. My father was converted during Conser's preaching at Timber Ridge Camp-meeting years ago. If *that's* the Yankee Preacher, our fun is up; I can't help.' Thus ludicrously or, to look at it in another light, providentially, the ducking scheme was frustrated and the company retired crestfallen to their homes."

It seems that this company was the fragment of a former military company, which had tried to re-organize for the purpose of ducking the preacher, but when they learned of his identity with the preacher Conser of former years they desired Capt. L——, to inform me that they had abandoned their unworthy project.

"Were any of the ducking party present when I preached that day?" I asked.

"Yes, quite a number. But I did not see Purcell or Wolf. They live quite a distance from here."

"Was Dr. J——, present?"

"Yes, and his wife was one of the women that shouted. The Doctor will not talk about it. I think he is ashamed; but he must keep in with the community. He knows you are right."

CHAPTER VI.

ECCENTRIC GENIUS.

In my wanderings through this mountainous country, I fell in with an eccentric genius who thought he knew more than all the world besides. He really was a careful and an extensive reader.

He invited me to his home and made me very welcome. His wife was a true Methodist and a loyal woman, and all the family were remarkably kind. The "major" (for who can not have a title in Virginia?) was a theologian and an expert disputant. He had a well stocked library for that locality. I always try to ingratiate myself with "mine host," by taking an interest in his affairs.

Accordingly, when I paid him a visit one day, I asked the major how much land he had. The greater part of his farm lay between two mountains, so that he might almost say, with the immortal Selkirk, "I am monarch of all I survey."

"Wall," he yawningly replied, "I have but a small farm now. My son has the other end, and I dunno jist how much is left, but thar is right smart still, p'raps some three thousand acres or thereabouts."

"Do you grow much tobacco?"

"Tobaccer! Wall, not much since the war. The war has spiled tobaccer, and all things else in this country;

even religion has declined since. But do you use tobaccer?"

"No, sir."

"Wall, I hearn that all Yanks used it. You're not a full Yank are ye?"

"No, sir, I am only a half-breed on that line."

"But whar you from and what on arth brought you in this wild country?"

"I am from Pennsylvania, and have come here to re-organize the old Methodist Episcopal Church."

"Why, we hearn the old Methodist Church had gone to sticks."

"Not quite, major."

"Still lives, does she? Will you form a class hereabouts?"

"Yes, if I can find some members."

"We'll find you one. My wife loves the old Church and says she will never go to a slavery church."

"Good for her! how about yourself, major?"

"Wall, I'm of no account; no good. I meddled in politics and slavery and lost my religion, for how can a slave-holder or a politician be a Christian?"

"Major, I give it up. Your position is too hard for me; still I would not say it is impossible."

"Be candid, we want no soft-soldering now. We had too much of that before the war. You preachers talked up, and preached up *slavery*, until you run us into rebellion, left us to fight it out, and then sneaked away. You all knowed slavery was wrong, but you were not honest enough to tell us so. What does Wesley say about slavery? And you *all* knowed slavery was wrong, but you preached it up to please us so as to get our good graces, and when we sold a slave you expected to get some of the money and good dinners. I tell you, you preachers were not honest. When a boy, I jined the Methodist Church. My father had slaves, but my mother always said it was wrong; but you preachers said it was right. I was fool enough to believe the preachers, and so I dabbled in slaves until I lost my religion, and my slaves, too. Thank God! the slaves are gone, but I am a little sorry for my religion."

"My dear major, I certainly sympathize with you, and I am sorry to confess that what you say is but too true; but still there were some honest preachers."

"Yes, my brother-in-law in Woodstock, told of one honest Methodist preacher. I think his name was 'Conser.' Did you ever know him?"

"Who is your brother-in-law in Woodstock?" I asked, evading his question.

"His name was Magruder."

"What, Dr. Magruder?"

"Yes, he was a doctor. Did you know him?"

"Why, I spent a whole Sunday with him years ago. How is the doctor?"

"O, he is dead long ago."

"I am sorry to hear that he is dead. He treated me very kindly."

"But what's the use to talk of slavery now; you preachers have done the mischief and ruined the church."

"What? ruined the church?"

"Yes, ruined it; filled it with slave-holders. I dare not tell you all about it, but you might find some of your class-leaders' and stewards' children in the cotton plantations in Georgia!! Such a church is no good."

"Major, I am ashamed to plead guilty to your awful charges; but the preachers are not the only ones to blame. The good book says, "Like people, like priest." When

Julius Cæsar looked on the slain after the battle that made him emperor, he wept and said, 'They would have it so.' So we say of you, *i. e.* your community, ' You would not listen to the truth.' Slavery, more properly legalized robbery, touched the sensitive nerve of the pocket-book and you chose preachers to your own liking, and now you complain. I have only to say sweep at your own door. But, major, let us forget the past and bury the shame of our fathers as did Shem and Japheth and learn wisdom from the folly of our ancestors. You and I will soon run our course. Let us not brood over the sins of the past, but now, while we may, prepare to meet our God." He pressed my hand and said, " Come see us the next time you are here," and I went on my way.

I have already intimated that I was almost universally known as the " Yankee Preacher." This opprobrious epithet, however, did me good ; it excited curiosity. No one cared for preacher Conser ; that was an old song ; but the " Yankee Preacher " was a novelty. Conser or any other preacher could be seen any day, but to see a " Yankee" was something new, and a " Yankee Preacher " a rare sight. So every one had to see and hear the " phenomenon," and crowds came wherever I preached. It was said that Judge E—— advised the people to stay away from the "Yankee Preacher " and he would soon leave. But curiosity got the better of this discretion, and they would come, some to hear, but more to see ; some from sympathy, but more from jealousy. I always avoided any allusion to the war or political subjects in my prayers or sermons; I had quite enough of these subjects at other times.

At Wesley Chapel I was called on to visit a man sick unto death. I told him who I was, and he appeared to be pleased ; confessed that during the war he had back-slidden, which impressed him he was wrong, and it impressed me so, too. He appeared very penitent and earnestly prayed for pardon; a few days after this he died. I was called on by his family to attend his funeral. The funeral was a large one, and I had many that day in my congregation that never before would come to hear me. Some expressed their opinion that if I was not a Southerner, I ought to be. I thought it best to do thorough work, as I went and tried to preach wherever I could get a congregation and collect members at least once a month. I intended to form classes and regular congregations and not simply let them for once see and hear a "Yankee Preacher."

What few loyal people were in this country that were not pitiful cowards, were brave indeed, and to meet a loyal preacher was to them a luxury, for which they hardly knew how to express their gratitude. An anti-slavery preacher many had never seen, especially among the younger ones, and then there were many anti-slavery women through this country, as there always were through all the South; and no wonder! Women too well knew the secret history of slavery not to abhor it. Alas, that they feared to express their abhorrence of that "sum of all villainies," even to their husbands. In many cases I was made a confident. There ever were but few religious women that did not abhor slavery.

CHAPTER VII.

DOMESTIC LIFE.

The domestic life of these people has always been simple, but especially so, during and since the war. Again and again some squad of Confederate soldiers would come and appropriate one-half of all they could find. Soon another squad would arrive and repeat the same process, so that unless they could conceal something beyond the search of the almost omniscient soldiers they would soon come to want.

When I came into this country in 1866, cattle, hogs, and sheep were rarities indeed. Large game, such as deer or bears was scarce, but rabbits, wood-chuck, raccoons and small game were plentiful, and these were substituted for domestic meats. Corn dodgers were always in order. In the mountains, when their owners could conceal them, there were some cows and horses. The table, as well as the wardrobe, felt the effect of the war. Flax, as in olden times, was grown, and the old spinning-wheel and hand loom were once more brought into requisition. There was no occasion for the preacher to lecture the sisters on their gayety. The war brought about more simplicity in apparel than the pulpit had ever done.

Wesley's high heads and enormous bonnets did not prevail here. Straw flats served for head-gear, and turkey wings for fans. The churches through the rural districts were dilapidated in the extreme, and frequently were inhabited by hogs, sheep and other animals, when not occupied by the "genus homo." Some were wholly deserted. The colored people, at best not remarkable for intelligence, were half crazed by their freedom, and in some localities allowed their emotions to impel them into the wildest fanaticism. They naturally were loyal to the Methodist Episcopal Church, and as naturally looked to me for moral advice and supervision. Of course, all colored people are spiritualists and firm believers in the most extreme supernatural. In their extravagant devotions they sometimes fell into trances and cataleptic fits and professed to see visions of angels and demons, and many of their departed masters in the dark regions reaping the reward of their cupidity in advocating and practicing slavery. All of which may have been true, but it was not proper to tantalize the living relatives by such revelations. I had no little trouble to check such fanaticism.

These spasmodic excesses were not confined to colored people. In various forms and divers places they had made their appearance, to the shame of those so affected, and the detriment of Christianity. Such fanaticism is encouraged by a class of zealots and divines of limited physical learning, and does in no way contribute to personal piety. Religious fervor uncontrolled by good common sense might be compared to a drunken locomotive running at large without an engineer to hold the throttle. A very wise writer says, "Be not righteous overmuch." Asceticism is of heathen origin, and is in no manner countenanced by Christ. All genuflections, fasts, vigils and mortifications are anti-Christian. It is only when professed Christians show to the irreligious that they are happy, not fanatical, that they commend Christianity to their acceptance.

CHAPTER VIII.

DISCOURAGED.

But I must again visit the White Church. I endeavored to arrange my appointments there not to interfere with the Southern preacher, while *he* made *his* arrangements for a less worthy purpose; in other words he made his appointment purposely to interfere with mine. I learned further that the rebels had a warrant in readiness to arrest me should I attempt to preach there. Squire B—— sent me word to call at his home on Saturday. I went and on Sunday morning he accompanied me to the church. He said the rebel preacher was to begin service a little in advance of time, so as to be engaged when I should appear. A crowd of the baser sort were to be stationed near the door, and as soon as I entered they were to hustle me out and the constable was to arrest me for causing a disturbance. How this could be done legally I could not understand, but the Squire remarked that that crowd cared little about the law and I had better prepare for the worst. When we arrived at the church they were singing, and the Squire asked me, 'shall we go in?' in such a plaintive tone that I perceived *he* would rather stay outside, so to avoid any disturbance I concluded not to enter. We were seen, however. The Squire then proposed to go and get dinner at Mr. K——'s, a man who had frequently declared he had been converted under my preaching. I, of course, expected

a warm reception! Imagine my surprise when Mr. K——
met us with most chilling manners. After a brief conversation, in which he never once alluded to such a thing as dinner, we retired in disgust. The Squire than escorted me to his sister's, where we were met cordially and where the inner man was abundantly refreshed. I took three members into church while at the home of the Squire's hospitable sister. I was to preach at three o'clock at an adjacent school house. Shortly before the hour the Squire and I again set out upon our travels. There was a chimney in a corner of the school-house and two men were trying to make a fire when we reached the place. Somehow they made more smoke than fire, so I preached in the cold to my *three* auditors and then, without supper, went to Piny Grove. Here I had a large congregation, a number of penitents at the altar and four converts; and so one of my saddest days ended well.

The revival at Piny Grove continued, and about forty persons were converted. During this winter we had an extensive revival at Wesley Chapel and at other places. I gathered up and recorded over one hundred good and true members in the old M. E. Church. All kinds of tales were circulated about me — some immoral, some ridiculous — all false. I treated all such opposition with silence. Apropos of "tails," I am reminded of an incident. The Wesley Chapel people were for the most part loyal and they had adhered to the old church. I was much pleased with their fidelity and did all for them that I could. Among other things we had a Fourth of July celebration, which gave much satisfaction. A good dinner was provided by the ladies, followed by a literary programme. One of the performers was a Sunday-school lad of ten years, who was quite a singer and an excellent mimic. He was to sing "Old

Daddy Grimes." He sang to the familiar tune of "Mears." Without a tremor in his voice and with a solemn sanctity in his looks, he reached the stanza:

> "The fox it has a bushy tail,
> The opossum's tail is *bar'* (bare),
> The raccoon's tail has rings all 'round,
> And frizzly is the *har* (hair)."

So comical was the performance and so original the pronunciation that the entire audience broke into a roar of laughter.

In the fall one of our converts at Wesley Chapel was taken with typhoid fever. Her name was Minerva P——. She was but sixteen years old, and, as was natural, she cherished a hope of recovery. But as her case became more and more serious her attachment to life became less. On one occasion she requested me not to pray for her recovery. I urged her not to despair of life, for she might live to be very useful; but she thought she might do more good when dead. She had an irreligious brother, older than herself, and she became impressed with the feeling that her death might be the means of saving him. What a noble, self-sacrificing spirit for one so young! Willing to give up her young life if by so doing her brother might be saved.

Presently her physician came, in company with a consulting physician. The sick girl expressed her regrets, saying, "I'm sorry they came; they can do me no good." The doctor sat by her side and said, "Minerva, do you think I can help you?"

"No, doctor; I do not want you to help me."

"Why, do you want to die?"

"Yes, I do, doctor. My Savior has called me, and I must go."

"Go where, my child?" said the doctor, deeply affected.

"Go to glory!" she exclaimed, and swooned away.

After a brief consultation, the doctor remarked to the mother, "Mrs. P——, we can do your daughter no good, and I will not call again." Soon after the doctors left, Minerva, having recovered sufficiently to speak, asked for her church certificate. They gave it to her. She held it with a trembling hand and then asked for her brother George. Geogre came into the room and said, "Sis, what do you want with me?"

The dying girl kissed the certificate and handing it to her brother said, "George accept this. It is all I have to leave you. I will never need it any more." And then with an angelic smile she added, "When you look at it think of me, and when you are tired of life come and see me. Will you?" She expired shortly after. But what a sermon she had preached to her irreligious brother. I do not know his subsequent history, but I feel sure that her words must have fallen as good seeds upon good ground.

But the end of my year drew nigh, and the time for me to leave. I had had hard work and poor pay, but I made many warm friends. The last interview I had at Wesley Chapel was an affecting one. Some who had at first done their utmost to drive me away, pressed my hand warmly at parting and begged my pardon. I sympathized with them, and freely forgave them.

CHAPTER IX.

STAUNTON.

In the year 1867, I was stationed at Staunton, Virginia. Presiding Elder Phelps thought I ought to go back to the James river section, but as I preferred not to go there again he did not insist upon it.

Staunton is a compact town of perhaps eight thousand inhabitants, well built but very irregular. If ever I was ostracized it was here, and if ever I felt its effects, it was in this semi-civilized community. The rebels had possession of our church, and the colored people had a church and preacher of their own, so I preached for a time in the theatre. My first congregation, including boys, numbered thirteen. The murky atmosphere of treason enveloped the town, and the people gave me a wide berth. Lucky for me, I was a Freemason. I soon visited a Lodge. Once in the Lodge I made the acquaintance of the most respectable portion of the community, and by them was politely treated and recognized socially thereafter. I soon obtained boarding with a prominent Freemason. He had quite a pretty daughter. This young lady had an admirer who happened to be a "Yankee" as they called all Northern people indiscriminately. One day in conversation with the father, I referred to the fact that his daughter's lover was a "Yankee." Mine host quickly replied, "Yes, but he is a good Democrat." I envinced some amusement at this recommendation, and he added, "O, well, it is different with you, for I think you are honest." I thanked him for the compliment.

While I still remained an object of dislike and suspicion to many of the inhabitants of Staunton, it was otherwise in the surrounding country. I soon had invitations to preach in the rural districts, and here I met not a few loyal Methodists. Among these people was a Mr. B——, a partial hypochondriac. When I called to see him, I discovered that he was more nervous than sick, and I tried to dispel his gloomy fears. He continually intimated that there was something dreadful in his case. I tried to laugh it off, but all in vain. Finally his wife left the room and we were alone for a few moments. He then said he would like to communicate to me a secret. I said I would hear anything not affecting the character of others. Then, drawing nearer to me, and with a tremor and a countenance that indicated almost the horrors of the damned, he whispered, "Bro. Conser, I have sinned against the Holy Ghost!"

Laying his hand upon his breast, he added, "O, I feel it here."

I at first made light of his remarks, but my curiosity became excited, and I finally asked what sin against the Holy Ghost he had committed. He replied solemnly, "*I voted for secession!*" I only wish others might have seen the sardonic look upon his countenance as he spoke. The scene would have been most ludicrous but for the fact that the man's mind was nearly unbalanced from brooding morbidly over his past conduct. I was heartily glad when his wife returned to the room, and I could get away.

CHAPTER X.

EMMA.

Several miles east of Staunton I met a family that for many years had been in the old Church, but in the whirlpool of excitement had been drawn into secession. One daughter, braver and more sensible than the rest, had kept a miniature star spangled banner in her possession, and professed her allegiance to the Methodist Episcopal Church all through the war.

It was through her that I became acquainted with the family. When she heard there was a Yankee preacher in Staunton, she hoped that he might be the representative of the church of her first love, and she determined to make his acquaintance. She invited me to visit her home, and agreed to make an appointment for me to preach in a school-house near by. She informed her mother of the fact, and received a sharp reprimand in reply. The circumstance came to her father's notice and he said, "Emma, did you tell the Sunday-school superintendent to make an appointment for the Yankee preacher?"

"I did, Pa," she answered.

"Well, where is he to stay over night?"

"Pa, I invited him to come here."

"You did! Who told you to do so?"

"Papa, I was converted in the old Methodist Episcopal Church and raised among the old Methodists, and I think you ought not to object to let me hear a preacher of the church I love. Pa, do you remember what you said to me the night I was converted?"

"No, Emma;" and he wiped his eyes.

"You said, 'Now, Emma, be faithful to your God and your church;' and I have tried to be so. The Methodist Episcopal Church has been the means of my conversion, and has never done me any harm; and I love her, and I am not ashamed of it. Papa, I thank you for the education you gave me; I can now teach school and earn my own living. I do not want to leave Ma—she is feeble; but, sooner than leave my church, I will leave my home. Only let me stay until the Yankee preacher comes, and I will pay you for entertaining him."

"Will you?" replied the old gentleman. "Emma, you are yet young," he continued, "and hardly competent to teach school, and, well—have you a kiss for your *penitent father?*" he added, with emotion.

Poor Emma! She could hardly cease crying long enough to kiss her father. After the exuberance of emotion was over, the father said, "My dear child, the *ice is broken*. I am with you. Your preacher is my preacher. Your church is my church. Too long have I cowered under the tyranny of popular sentiment; I never was a secessionist at heart, and I always loved the Old Church, but I was afraid. I would to Heaven I had been as brave as you; but it is over now. Yes, Emma, I'll go with you to hear the 'Yankee Preacher,' and you'll introduce me, and I'll invite him to my house; and while I have a home, you and the old side preacher shall have a home, too."

At this juncture the old lady commenced shouting, "Glory, Glory to God! Is it possible that others think as I think, and feel as I feel? Why, Pa, I always believed secession was wrong, and the Old Church was right, and

Emma was right; but I was afraid to say what I thought, and when I scolded Emma for inviting her preacher here, I knew I did wrong. Emma, can you forgive a sorrowing mother?" Before Emma could speak, the old lady began shouting again, "Glory, Glory to God! I am once more free! And now, father, give me your hand, and go with me to the Methodist Episcopal Church, and let Emma's preacher come here as in the olden times."

The history of this family is the secret history of many.

CHAPTER XI.

UPHILL WORK.

Several miles from the place mentioned in the preceding chapter, I arranged to hold a protracted meeting. I had several members in the vicinity. The only available place for holding our meeting was a spare room in a private house. The house was long, and the room we occupied was rather capacious. I intended to commence the services on Saturday, but no one came, and then it began to rain in the evening. Sunday morning opened dreary, indeed. I had announced Love Feast at nine o'clock A. M., and went to our extemporized church to find no one there, and no fire. One of the friends who accompanied me collected some wet wood and attempted to build a fire in the large fire-place. We applied the matches to his wet chips, but, although he blew himself warm, he only blew the matches out. All the surroundings were so unpleasant that I contemplated adjourning the meeting and returning to Staunton. By and by, however, the fire commenced to burn and the people began to arrive. Before eleven o'clock the extemporized church was well filled, and we had a good service. On our way to dinner Mr. D—— remarked "that the prospects were promising for a good revival." I never saw prospects more unpromising, but I did not say so. At night our little chapel was crowded, and a blazing fire in the huge fire-place afforded both heat and light. It was difficult for me to obtain standing-room without encroaching on the hearth, which for divers reasons I did not like to do. I invited mourners, and a goodly number presented themselves, and a good revival resulted.

A sad occurrence transpired in this community, and during this meeting. Among the converts was a young girl subject to epilepsy. A few days after her conversion, in an epileptic fit, she fell into the fire and was burned to death. We took her corpse into the church, where, a few brief hours before, she had been converted. In my remarks I emphasized the fact that God always converts through human agencies, and urged upon my audience the importance of youthful piety, from the fact that God wishes us to be not only good but also useful. And then we sang this solemn and appropriate hymn:

"Must I go, and empty-handed
Thus my dear Redeemer meet;
Not a day of service given him,
Lay no trophies at his feet?"

The poor girl had a short religious experience, and we had a very solemn time at her funeral. I think this circumstance helped me in that community, for it minified things temporal and magnified things eternal.

In my ministerial utterances I studiously avoided any allusion to sectional disputes; so much so, that a prominent gentleman remarked that as a preacher the Yankee Preacher was much like other people, and if let alone would make no disturbance.

CHAPTER XII.

"TOBE."

On one occasion, as I was walking in the country, I came where there was an old dilapidated dwelling which might have seen better times in ante bellum days. As I approached, the occupant of the house called his dog—a spaniel—seized him by the neck and began kicking him vigorously in the side with his heavy brogans. The poor brute howled piteously, and the *other brute* swore like a colonel. As I drew nearer, I exclaimed:

> "Let dogs delight to bark and bite,
> For 'tis their nature to;
> Let bears and lions growl and fight,
> For God has made them so;
> But, neighbor, you should never let
> Such angry passions rise,
> Your big brogans were never made
> To kick your spaniel's side."

The infuriated man looked around and said, "D——n the dog; I'll kill him!" still holding on to his neck. I inquired the cause of his excitement, when his wife came out and said, "Joe is more to blame than Tobe. The fact is, Joe has been on a spree, and when he came home late last night he tried to fool with Tobe. It was dark, and Tobe thought it was a thief; for Joe would not speak, and so Tobe wouldn't let him inside the gate until Joe said 'Tobe.' Then Tobe was friendly. I don't think Tobe is to blame."

The man was still drunk, I perceived. But I spoke to him, and asked if what his wife said was true. Joe admitted that he was just trying Tobe's pluck, as he called it, and again commenced swearing and kicking the poor dog. I now became excited, and said, "Joe, quit that! Why, that was noble in Tobe, and you should caress and not beat him for his fidelity. Meantime, from some cause, Joe's hand began to bleed, and poor Tobe tried to lick the blood from his tormentor's hand. Here the brutal man began kicking again. My ire was up.

"Now," said I, "kick him again and I'll kick you;" and I called the dog to me. But Tobe looked piteously at me, and again licked his master's hand. Meanwhile, Joe's wife seemed much interested in the "stranger." She whispered something to Joe, who by this time commenced sobering up. Joe turned to me and said, "I say, stranger, come in and have some dinner."

"Joe, do you mean it?" I asked.

"Why, my wife said I should."

The lady blushed and retired. Joe and I then entered the house and sat down to discuss the advantages and disadvantages of temperance. While we were thus occupied, I overheard the following colloquy in the adjoining room where Joe's good wife was preparing dinner: "Say, Mattie (a girl of perhaps ten years), run down to the stable and get some eggs. Be quick now."

Mattie hurried off to the stable and soon returned with the doleful message, "Why, mamma, there isn't none but one nest-egg in the nest, and there are plenty of hens standing around doin' nothin'." Mattie evidently thought that hens, like other folks, should be up and doing. I need not add that my hopes of a good dinner were seriously modified. By and by the kind lady—for she was a lady, far superior to her husband and her surroundings—entered the room and in a sweet, gentle tone, said, "Gentlemen, please come to dinner." Joe at once jumped up and said, "Come, stranger, and have a bite." And so, Joe leading the way, I followed, and we sat down to a nice dinner. Joe looked a little confused. The wife glanced at me and nodded her head, as much as to say, "Please say prayers." This was a surprise, but what surprised me more, was to see a plate of temptingly fried eggs. Where these eggs came from was a mystery, and as I was too polite to inquire, the matter remains a mystery to this day.

CHAPTER XIII.

PERSONAL DEVILS.

I had a friend in Staunton, Dr. T——, with whom I used to converse on theological subjects. On one occasion he insisted on my giving the people of Staunton a lecture on demonology and witchcraft. I hesitated, because I thought no one cared to hear the "Yankee Preacher." But the doctor insisted that my ostracism was official, and by no means personal, and that he had always heard my name mentioned respectfully, except when national or ecclesiastical matters were referred to, and that while I had but few ecclesiastical, I certainly had many personal friends. He was anxious to know whether I was a Freemason, because he had heard several Freemasons speak highly of me; and, said the doctor, "When you have the Masons on your side, you have the best people in Staunton." He assured me that such a lecture from me would draw a crowd; but still I declined. He then wished me to deliver my views in his office on that occult subject. I told him I would, perhaps, on to-morrow night, as I was in a hurry just then. The next night I was at his office and he introduced me to Professor R——, whose lecture on psychology I had heard. The professor inquired, "Mr. Conser, the doctor informs me that you sometimes lecture on witchcraft. Will you be so kind as to deliver that lecture here?"

"No, professor, I would rather not," I said.

"Well, as a Christian minister, you certainly believe in the existence of devils and witches."

"Professor, you appear to be more certain of my belief than I am myself."

"Well, Mr. Couser, is not the Christian bible full of devils and witches?"

"That indefinite question I might answer both affirmatively and negatively."

"How is that?"

"Well, that depends on the meaning and definition of terms. That you are either tall or small depends on the objects of comparison. That the terms Satan (Hebrew), Diabolos (Greek), occur I know very well; but what these terms mean is quite another matter. I am by no means certain that the Hebrew *Hasatan*, or the Greek *Diabolos*, or our English term *Devil*, mean a physical hideous monster with cloven feet and barbed tail."

"Mr. Couser, do you understand Hebrew?"

"I have tried to understand a little of Biblical Hebrew."

"What is the meaning of the Hebrew word Satan?"

"Satan is not a Hebrew word," I said. "It is a Hebrew word anglicised."

"What is the Hebrew word?"

"The Hebrew is *Hasatan* or *Shaitan*, and literally means an adversary indifferent as to character."

"What do you mean by indifferent as to character?"

"I simply mean that the term *Hasatan*, anglicised *Satan*, has no moral meaning, and may be used either in a good or a bad sense."

"Is the Hebrew word *Hasatan* ever used in a good sense?"

"I think it is, in Numbers xxii. 22."

"Well, do you pretend to say there is no personal devil?"

"By no means. For aught I know, there may be legion; but I do say I have never seen any, except the pretty girls."

"The what?"

"The pretty girls. Let me illustrate. While stationed in Northern Pennsylvania I was occasionally called on to attend weddings, and although temperance was popular, still it was considered permissible to drink wine at weddings. I, however, always declined. A certain lady, without my knowledge, of course, boasted that she would have me drink wine at her wedding. In time I was called on to perform her marriage ceremony. Now, this lady was one of the most conspicuous in the place, and she was to be married to the cashier of the bank. You know the officiating minister is quite a factor on such occasions, and can augment or detract from the convivial enjoyments thereto pertaining. I therefore resolved to make myself as agreeable as circumstances would allow; the more so, as I expected a nice fee for my brief services. A gay company was present, the marriage ceremony passed off satisfactorily, and then the wine was freely indulged in. Presently, the pretty bride, with several attendants, approached me and insisted that I should drink her health and happiness. "With great pleasure," I replied, and I took up a glass of water. The bride protested, and insisted that I should drink wine with her if with no one else. In an undertone I playfully declined. Still she persisted. I did not wish to attract the attention of the jovial audience, and still hesitated. At last she declared that a refusal on my part to drink wine with her would be considered a personal offense! I now had only one way left to extricate myself from the predicament into which she (this adversary or Satan) had crowded me. I looked her full in the face, and, addressing her by the new name I had just given her, I said, "Mrs. W——, I thought you were my friend."

"I *am* your friend, and I think I have shown it," she replied, with some surprise.

"And yet you want me to do an act that would disgrace me in time, and, perhaps, damn me throughout eternity?"

"Why, Mr. Conser, you frighten me;" and her face suddenly became very grave.

"Mrs. W——, I am the sworn friend of the Lord Jesus Christ, and to comply with your request would be an infraction of my oath. If I can retain your friendship only at such a price, I can not for a moment hesitate—*I can not drink that wine!*"

Her eyes filled with tears, she grasped my hand and earnestly begged my pardon. In spite of my efforts to the contrary, our dialogue *did* attract attention, and I was forced to explain what had happened. I said, "The wine, ladies and gentlemen, is a small factor in this case. It is the force of example. Drinking that wine might disgust *you*, but a child or grandchild might learn the fact and think or say, 'My grandfather was a good man, and *he* drank wine at weddings,' and God only knows whereunto this incident might lead." One of the directors of the bank remarked, "Mr. Conser, you need make no apologies. It would be well if we all took such comprehensive views of the subject."

For a few moments the company was sobered, but soon the gayety was resumed and the evening passed merrily away. I lost no fee, and best of all, no friends, by maintaining my principles. This was one of the severest temptations of my life, and beautifully illustrates the meaning of the Hebrew *Hasatan*. In this particular instance we came in conflict or were adversaries to each other without any moral turpitude on either side. I say again, "the worst devils are the *pretty girls.*"

"All that may be true, but you certainly know the New Testament is full of the possession of devils," said the professor.

"Professor, you, as a Greek scholar, certainly know that your language is very equivocal."

"Well, it's the language of the bible," he retorted.

"What Bible? Certainly not the Greek. *Demoniacs*, or *those possessed*, were not possessed with *Satans*, but *Demons* — a very different order of beings — supposed order, I might say; for I believe them to be imaginary! The account given of their origin, in the apocryphal books of Enoch, is certainly mythical. As for witchcraft, thank God! like pagan mythology, it can not endure the test of intellectual investigation."

"But, Bro. Conser, you certainly know that the bible is full of witches and witchcraft."

"No, professor; I know no such thing. I do know, however, that such terms occur there, but the ideas are entirely different. Biblical witchcraft and modern or heathenish witchcraft are as different as a May rose is from an Arctic iceberg. Witches in the bible were simply fortune-tellers, and were put under interdiction because they abused their superior knowledge by imposing on their more ignorant neighbors. Such a witchcraft as a combination with the devil and the possession of supernatural powers is never mentioned in the bible."

"How about the witch of Endor?" he queried.

"The witch of Endor was simply a fortune-teller, and had no more to do with Samuel than you or I have."

"But did she not bring up the ghost of Samuel?"

"Professor, there is not a word in the narrative about any ghost, and you have no authority to interject it."

"Well, was not Samuel there?"

"No, sir; Saul was there."

"But did not Saul converse with Samuel?"

"No, sir; Saul conversed with a ventriloquist personating Samuel."

"Then you think demons and witches are heathen superstitions?"

"Most assuredly," was my reply.

Our conversation then drifted into materialism and fatalism, and we had not half exhausted this highly interesting theme when I was forced by the lateness of the hour to excuse myself and retire to my home.

CHAPTER XIV.

A SEVERE TEST.

There was a small village near Staunton called W— B—. It contained a tavern, a store, a blacksmith shop, and a few scattered houses. It also had, at this time, a neat little Methodist Church, which owed its existence largely to the following circumstances:

It had been the boast, some years previous, that there was not a religious person in W— B—. At this period in the moral history of W— B—., the following incident occurred: A Miss B—— obtained a situation there as school-teacher. This young lady improved a vacation by attending a *bush meeting* in the neighborhood, during which she became impressed with the propriety of making her peace with God. Sympathizing friends gave her what instruction they could, but to no purpose; her state of mind became apparently worse and worse. A pious minister obtained an interview. The young lady informed the minister that she was teaching in W— B— and wished to make her peace with God.

"And are you willing to give up anything and do anything God may require?" asked the minister.

"I certainly am," she replied.

"Well, Miss B——, suppose God were to require you to open or close your school with prayer, would you be willing to do it?"

"I can not do that, because the community is entirely irreligious and I would at once lose my situation."

"And that may be the secret of your present embarrassment," said the preacher. "So you are willing to do all but *that*. But God accepts no divided services."

"Do you mean to say that I can not be religious without praying in my school."

"No, Miss; all I mean to say is, if you *sincerely believe* that God wants you to do so, will you do it?"

She hesitated a moment and then said, "I will, God helping me." It was enough. The consecration was complete, and as such accepted, and peace and joy resulted.

But the time came for her school to re-open and with it came the impression that she must have prayers. All was auspicious. The day was pleasant and the attendance good. Finally the lessons had all been rehearsed and the time for closing school arrived. With a quaking heart the young teacher arose and said: "Children, when I dismiss the school, you can all go home right away, but if any of you will stay with me a few minutes, we will read a lesson from the Bible and have prayers." This took them all by surprise and they *all* remained. The exercises were brief, but all appeared pleased at the "new departure" and some seemed much impressed.

There lived in W— B— a Mr. M——, who was magistrate, store-keeper and school trustee. He was the chief man of the town, and was looked to in every emergency. This Mr. M—— had a little daughter, some twelve years of age, who was an attendant at Miss B——'s school. On her return from school that afternoon the little girl said, "O papa! you should just have been at school this evening. Oh! we all cried, and were awful sorry."

"What did you all cry about?" queried the father.

Then she rehearsed the circumstances of Miss B——'s reading, and singing, and praying. This was sad and bad news to the squire; so the next day he held a consultation with another of the trustees, and it was finally agreed upon that the squire should admonish Miss B—— to quit her religious freaks or close her school. The following morning he sent a note to the teacher by his little daughter, asking her to call at his home in the evening. Miss B—— too well suspected his object, but she came as he had requested.

"Well, Miss B——, they say you have commenced a religious revival in your school; how is this?"

"Squire, I have attended to all my school duties. I have regularly dismissed the school, announcing that those who wished could stay for prayers. Have I neglected any of my duties in so doing?"

"None whatever, Miss B——. But you know the sense of this community. We want no religious fanaticism here. Miss B——, you must either quit your fanaticism or quit your school," was the reply.

"Squire, I suppose you mean by my fanaticism, my religion."

"Yes, I suppose you call it religion," was his gruffy response.

"Well, if I must quit either my religion or my school, I suppose I must quit my school. When shall I close?" the poor girl asked with trembling voice.

"Friday evening," and he left the room.

Poor Miss B——! With a heavy heart she walked down the road towards her boarding place. All the other schools in the district were taken, and what to do for a living she did not know. Friday afternoon came. Again she requested the children to remain for prayers if they felt so disposed. After reading a short lesson she prayed for the children, for her persecutor, and then while all were on their knees, she sang:

>"Jesus, I my cross have taken,
>All to leave and follow the," etc.

Meantime the squire's daughter became greatly affected and suddenly throwing her arms around her teacher's neck, kissed her and begged her not to quit the school, saying:

" O, teacher, I love Jesus! I love Jesus!"

But the school was closed. The squire's daughter hurried home. She met her father in the hall and exclaimed, " O, papa, papa, I love Jesus! I love Jesus!"

The squire was taken by surprise, and before he could speak, his happy daughter said:

"Papa, will you promise me one thing?"

"What is it my child?"

"Well, promise first."

Almost instinctively he said, "Yes, I will." Then, taking him by the hand, she led him up-stairs to her room and said, "Now, papa, I want you to get on your knees and pray until you love Jesus as I do." As if pressed by an iron hand, the squire fell rather than kneeled and began to pray, "God, be merciful to me, a sinner." Soon the mother came up, and then the little girl's brother. And in a few moments she had three mourners on their knees. The dear child, like an angel, kept flying from one to the other begging them to love Jesus. No one in the little company thought of supper just then. Presently the squire expressed a desire to see the young school-teacher. Some one went to her boarding-place and said, "Miss B——, squire M—— wants to see you immediately." She was then busy packing her trunk, but she obeyed the summons and started for the squire's mansion. As she walked along she thought, "What on earth can the old tyrant want with me now? He has driven me from my school, and, perhaps, to the poor-house. Oh! it is too hard. But God will help me to love even an enemy." As she entered the house the little girl met her teacher in the doorway and cried, "O Miss B——, I think papa loves Jesus, and I am so happy, so happy! Walk up to the room." True enough, the little girl had guessed the truth. The squire had found peace, and when the young teacher approached him he said, "Miss B——, I dare not, but I would like to kiss you! God bless you a thousand times! Miss B——, have you got religion enough to forgive me? You know Saul was as bad as I, and he was pardoned." "Why, certainly, squire. Though you have driven me from my school, I pity you much more than I blame you," was the noble answer.

"Miss B——, I propose to call a meeting of the school trustees to-morrow morning. Will you be present, too?"

"If you desire it."

On Saturday morning the trustees met, reversed their act of cruelty, and begged Miss B—— to resume her school on Monday, with the distinct understanding that she might have full liberty to introduce any religious services into her school that she pleased.

CHAPTER XV.

A SNAKE STORY.

My way being hedged about in Staunton, I spent much of my time in the country. My Presiding Elder, E. P. Phelps, frequently sent me out on his district while he attended to my work in Staunton. In this way I traveled over much of the ground I had occupied the former year. The topography of all that country is rugged, though the valley is fertile. My accommodations, though genial, were often quite rustic; straw and leaves, gathered in the woods, served as mattresses, and wooden troughs as wash bowls. A large comb suspended from a nail by a long string served for a whole family. Acorns were frequently used as a substitute for coffee, and mountain herbs for tea. The army-worm had crawled all over this country, and the remaining inhabitants had not recovered from its dire effects. What loyal people there were, not cowed by the tyranny of conventional rules, received me with open arms and made me as happy as they possibly could.

Much of my time was spent among mountains infested with snakes. I had a natural antipathy to these repulsive reptiles and I feared them exceedingly. On one occasion in the dead of winter (when snakes are not as a rule roaming around) I passed the night with some friends who lived in the mountains. A thoughtful member of the family placed a warm brick in my bed, for there was no fire in the room. I retired in good season. After disrobing I hurriedly jumped into bed, when to my horror my foot came in contact with something warm, which I instantly concluded was a huge snake coiled up! With a yell, I sprang at least ten feet from the bed at one leap! The house shook, the windows rattled, the water splashed from the pitcher on the stand, and altogether I made a great racket. The lady below hearing the uproar, came rushing to my door and cried: "Mr. Conser, Mr. Conser, what is the matter?"

"Oh Mrs. M——!" I shouted "there is a snake in my bed."

"A snake! Can it be possible?" she exclaimed.

For a moment there was silence. Then I heard a ripple of laughter and Mrs. M—— softly said, "I wonder if it isn't the warm brick?"

I had not another word to say, but crept quietly back to bed and for very shame covered my face and went to sleep.

CHAPTER XVI.

FAIRFAX.

In the spring of 1868 my time at Staunton expired, and I asked to be placed nearer to Baltimore, where my family was. Bishop Ames accordingly sent me to Fairfax, in sight of Washington City. Here I was entirely separated from the Secessionists. Northern people were numerous, and a goodly number of native Virginians were loyal. Several years had now passed since the war closed, and the church was pretty well reorganized. The few rebels I encountered seemed sour. They still smarted under the mortification of defeat. The country around Fairfax had a God-forsaken look. Here the armies of both sections had swayed to and fro, leaving destruction and desolation in their path. Here with McClellan's army I had lain (I was chaplain of the Fifth Pennsylvania Reserve Corps) all the fall and winter of 1861-62, held at bay by *Quaker cannon at Manassas.

During my year at Fairfax I was entertained on one occasion by Bro. A——, one of the members of our congregation.

Soon after tea he adroitly turned the conversation to nautical subjects. He inquired:

" Bro. Conser, were you ever on the high seas?"

" Only once, Bro. A——."

---

*Quaker cannon were simply painted logs, imitating cannon,

" Well, do you know anything about pirates? "

" Nothing but what I may have read."

" But I do," eagerly replied Bro. A——.

" Were you ever on the ocean?" I inquired.

" O, yes, many a time, and among pirates, too."

And then he narrated his adventures among pirates that utterly surprised me.

"Once upon a time," he went on, "as the merchantman aboard of which I was, passed near the Isle of Pines, we were chased by a pirate. The captain put on all sail and tried to escape; but in vain. The pirates soon approached. The captain then ordered all hands on deck, and ordered a fight to the death should the pirates attempt to board our vessel. Among the passengers was a Quaker who could not conscientiously fight, so when the pirates boarded our ship the Quaker ran down a hatchway. The pirate pursued him, and as he ran up on deck again to escape them, one of the villains grabbed the Quaker and was about to throw him overboard, when the Quaker hit the pirate a blow that laid him flat upon the deck. Then another pirate grappled with the Quaker. Finally the Quaker got the advantage, and pitched his assailant overboard. By this time the pirate who had been felled to the deck recovered somewhat from his blow and made a dash for the Quaker. He, too, after a brief struggle, was thrown into the yawning waves. By and by we succeeded in fighting the pirates off, and when all became calm again, the captain said to the Quaker:

"I thought you Quakers wouldn't fight?"

"Well," replied the brave Quaker, "thee knows I should not have done so, if they had stayed on their own ship."

"Did you ever fall in with Captain Kidd?" I inquired, somewhat quizzically, I confess.

"Well—yes. Do you know anything about Captain Kidd?"

"Nothing but what I have read."

"Captain Kidd was a bad man," he declared.

"I suppose all pirates are bad," said I.

"Well, yes, but there is a difference. Did you know Gibbs and Wansley?"

"I once saw them hung in effigy."

"In what?" with an inquiring look.

"Effigy. Why, I have been hung in effigy twice."

"Did it hurt much?"

"It may have hurt the effigy, but it did not hurt me."

In this vein we conversed the entire evening.

The next day after this conversation, I called upon a neighbor of Bro. A——'s. On learning that I had spent the night preceding with Bro. A——, he said, "Did he tell you his pirate stories?"

"Stories? He told me of his adventures upon the high seas."

"Bro. Conser, do you know that Bro. A—— has never been on the sea at all?"

"Is that so?" I replied, with astonishment.

"Why, sir, all those piratical stories are imaginary."

"But he narrated these incidents as *facts*, and you say they are *false*," I returned.

"I do not say they are false, but I do say, as far as Bro. A—— is concerned, that he never saw a pirate."

"Then he lied to me shamefully. And do you have such men in your church here?" said I, indignantly.

"Bro. Conser, Bro. A—— is one of our best members. You will never catch him in a lie or other crime, excepting his mania for telling piratical tales. He may have read these tales in his younger days, and, by repeating them often, at last has come to believe that the adventures he narrates were really his own. With him this is a weakness, not a wickedness. You could not get a committee that would find Bro. A—— guilty of falsehood; he is too good a man."

I could but commend the charitable vindication of a weak brother's faults by his neighbor.

CHAPTER XVII.

BORN OF WATER.

One day, as I was waiting for the train at Arlington Station, an ex-slave approached, and, with a smile that indicated sociability, said, "Good evenin', sar."

I returned the salutation.

"Gwine to Falls Church, mister?" he asked.

"Uncle, I am going to Herndon, beyond Falls Church."

"Des ye live at Herdin?"

"No, uncle; I live in Baltimore."

"W'at is ye gwine to Herdin for?"

"I expect to preach there to-morrow, uncle."

"Is ye a pritcher?"

"I am."

"A Baptis' pritcher?"

"No, uncle; I am a Methodist preacher."

"D——n the Met'dis' preacher."

"Why, why, uncle! Do you use profane language?"

"Ugh! Dat nuthin'. I do wuss dan dat."

"But that is wicked, uncle."

"Ugh! You d——n Met'dis' preacher say so, but it ain't, nuther."

"Uncle, do you profess to have religion?"

"Yes, sir; right smart."

"And still you use such bad words?"

"Mister, 'scuse me. I'se so used to dat word dat I can't help sayin' it. I mean no respecs; Lord knows, I don't."

"Well, but such words are unbecoming a Christian. Doesn't your conscience upbraid you?"

"Now massy, you talk 'bout conscience. Ise know all about conscience. When I was a boy I 'tended a Met'dis' camp-meetin' and de brederen 'suaded me to get 'ligion an' I tried hard, but I was jis givin' up, an' den it come all at once, and O! I make an awful fuss! Then my conscience was tender jus' like a baby's an' all de time botherin' me, and I daren' say no hard words, and say no wite lies, and hook no chickens, and drink no grog, so I jus' let 'ligion go, and tried to cult'vate conscience to be stronger, and not weak and tender like baby's. 'Cause you know conscience can be cultivated like 'backer."

"But why let your religion go?"

"'Cause Methodis' 'ligion no good. Won't stay nohow. Jis as de war begin, I said, Bob (my Baptis' name, Robert Lee) I says 'Bob you better get ligion, cause you may go to de war too, and may be killed. So better get 'ligion fust, but not Met'dis' 'ligion—dat won't stick.' So I tried Baptis' 'ligion, and was born again of water, an' the spirit, an' dat stick good."

"So your Baptist religion sticks good. But how about using such profane words?"

"'Fane words! I use no 'fane words."

"Why, Bob, did you not say 'd—n' several times in my presence?"

"Dat no 'fane word."

"But no Christian should use such words. Does not your conscience upbraid you."

"Dar, you Met'dis' blind leadin' de blind. You can do nothin' but conscience bothers you. Why does you not cultivate conscience? When I was born of water and de spirit, conscience tried hard to bother me again. I was jis like a little chile. But Paul says, 'Put away childish things.' Den I tried some bad words. At fust conscience tried to —what do you call dat big word—'uproad?'

"No Bob, I said ' upbraid.' "

"O, yes! now I ' member. Well, as I was sayin', conscience tried to upbraid me for usin' such words, but I kep' on cultivatin' conscience, till it got strong and manly-like."

"Is your conscience strong enough now to steal poultry, tell white lies, etc?"

"Well, yes; 'pend much on cir'stances."

"When you said you were born again of water and the spirit, what did you mean by being born of water?"

"Good grashus! You knows Ise 'mersed in de water."

"You were immersed in water, and that you call ' being born again of water and the spirit?'"

"Zackley so. Caze ' mersion is the true baptism."

"But why is immersion the only true baptism?"

"Caze the Greek always mean ——— 'mersion."

"Can you read Greek, Bob?"

"No, massy. But I understan' de Greek langwidge."

"You do!"

"Why, bless de Lord! De Greek is de Baptis' langwidge."

"Indeed! But how you can understand the Greek language when you can not read, I can not see."

"Well, the parson understands Greek, an' he tells us."

"So you have the parson's word for it. But suppose he knows no more Greek than you do?"

"He says he knows all about it."

"My dear Bob, that is easily said."

"I knowd he never went to college! But did Christ ever go to college?"—this with a triumphant air.

"I do not think he needed to go."

"All college men is not good men—is they?"

"I suppose not. Nor are all ignoramuses good men. But how much water had you when you were immersed?"

"All the 'tomac!"

"All the Potomac! My dear sir, you had quite too much water for the amount of spirit in your baptism. The next time you are 'born again of water and the spirit,' please take less water and more spirit to rid yourself of such black spots as swearing, lying, stealing and drinking rum; for water, evidently, can not wash them away."

Just then the train approached. Bob entered the first car, I the second, and we met no more.

CHAPTER XVIII.

ARMY REMINISCENCES.

While at Fairfax, I had abundant opportunity to visit my home in Baltimore, and on the whole the year was prosperous and pleasant. But my health, which had been seriously impaired in the Chickahominy swamps during McClellan's siege of Richmond, began to fail. I could no longer do effective work as an itinerant Methodist preacher, and at the close of my year at Fairfax I retired from the active ministry.

I am proud to say that I was always an anti-slavery man. During all the exciting time, from the enactment of the fugitive slave law until actual hosilities commenced in 1861, in my pulpit and every where I preached what I practised, loyalty to God, church and country. I was quite too loyal for the semi-rebs of Baltimore, and the church authorities saw proper to remove me in 1860, from Baltimore to Huntington, Pa. After the bombardment of Fort Sumter I went to Washington, and through Gen. Cameron (then Secretary of War) offered my services to my country. Gen. Cameron, whom I had known for many years, wishing probably to favor me, asked whether I would not prefer a post-chaplaincy. I replied that if I had a choice I would prefer going to the front; I had come from a patriotic family, and did not wish to be hid in a fort. He sent me home to await orders. While waiting to hear from the Secretary of War, all my leisure time from my ministerial work was occupied with Senator Scott in recruiting; I finding the recruits, and Senator Scott taking care of them until called for. Hon. A. G. Curtin, Governor of Pennsylvania had organized a corps of volunteers known as the Reserve Corps of Pennsylvania Volunteers. Two regiments of this corps, the "5th" and "Buck-tails" had been ordered to West Virginia early in the summer of 1861. Immediately after the Bull Run disaster, this corps was called for by the United States. The two regiments beyond Cumberland were ordered to report at Harrisburg, Penn., and they returned through Huntingdon. Here I joined the "5th," and accompanied them to Washington as chaplain. We were camped in the vicinity of Washington from August, 1861, to March, 1862, with an army of nearly 200,000 troops, held at bay by the Quaker cannon before referred to.

On Thanksgiving day, Col. Simmons requested me to make a patriotic address to our regiment. Accordingly the regiment deployed into a hollow square around a small platform extemporized for the occasion. The officers of the regiment occupied the platform, and our regimental colors supplied all the decoration required. In the course of my address I called attention to that flag and remarked: "It is blue, but not boosled with rum; it is spotted, but not with crime; it is red, but it has never been stained with innocent blood; it is white, but not palsied with fear; it bears the stripes, but it has never been whipped." Here my voice was completely drowned by the shouts of the battalion and I left the stage.

Oh! how grieved I was to see that flag, afterwards riddled by rebel bullets, shot by those who once had kissed it!

In March, 1862, we broke camp on Arlington, and were marched to Manassas, where we had full opportunity to examine the *dangerous* (?) Quaker cannon that held McClellan in awe so long. From Manassas we marched to

Fredericksburg, which we easily captured. We camped on Mary's Hill, which Gen. Burnside failed to take. From Fredericksburg we embarked on a rickety steamer, and were sent to the Peninsula to re-inforce McClellan's army. We landed at the White House (Fitzhugh Lee's), thirty-four miles east of Richmond. From this point we were sent by rail to the famous Chickahominy. Here we began our march to Mechanicsville, six miles north of Richmond; and on the 27th of June we were repelled by the overwhelming rebel guns. I came very near being captured that day. We were camped on the east bank of a small stream east of Mechanicsville. Our battalion was on picket that day beyond the town, but I remained in camp. After dinner I took my hammock and went into a grove by the little run. Tying my hammock to the trees, I got into it, fell asleep, and dreamed of a thunder-storm. What I, in my dream, believed to be a thunder-storm proved in reality to be cannonading; and before I could recover my senses, our troops came running pell-mell past me and rallied just beyond where I had been sleeping. By the time I was fully awake I was just between the two armies, a conspicuous target for both. Fortunately, the rebels halted on the west bank of the run. They immediately commenced firing. I sprang from my hammock and ran to the rear of our troops, where we all lay flat upon the ground. Our men were ordered to hold their fire. Now, if there is a painful position in a battle, it is to be shot at without permission to return the compliment. But soon the time came, and the order was given to fire. The "Johnnies" attempted to cross the stream between us, but we held them at bay. The scene was appalling. It appeared to me that no sacrifice of men could check the rebels. Our men were brave, however, and held their ground. It was a drawn battle. Both armies remained upon the field that night, sleeping upon their arms. Early on the morning of the 28th we retreated to Gaines' Hill, a few miles down the Chickahominy. There we had a severe battle, and lost heavily, especially our artillery. We began to realize that we had demons to encounter. War is essentially barbarous. The nearer the savage, the better the soldier. You commend the soldier for his bravery, but civilians are not good judges of bravery in a soldier. None more brave than a coward when he must fight. Fighting is purely mechanical. The soldier in battle has not time to calculate causes and effects. Like a fisticuff, when you are struck, you want to strike back. Right or wrong is a matter for after consideration. The ranks of an army are just so many machines. How a Christian can pray for his enemies and then shoot them dead, indifferent whether he sends them to heaven or hell, I do not understand. The battle-field is no place for Christians!

As chaplain of the battalion I belonged to the colonel's staff, and during a battle should have been a certain number of paces on his left in the rear, but I always volunteered to carry wounded from the front, which would bring me often between both armies, and in danger from both. I found it no sinecure position to carry or drag men wounded and helpless back through our ranks. On Monday, during that seven days' battle at Turkey Bend, our corps was on the extreme left. We were vigorously attacked and we as vigorously defended our position. Our temporary regimental hospital was under a clump of trees in the rear of the regiment. Dr. Donaldson, assistant surgeon, asked me to hold a wounded soldier while he attempted to extract a bullet from his neck. I held him under his arms, his head resting on my shoulder and I kneeling on my right knee. While thus engaged, the rebels flanked us on the left and began shelling our extemporized hospital. Dr. Donaldson was busily working to secure the bullet, when suddenly a shell exploded near by us and one of the flying pieces lodged in my left thigh. The surgeon sprang up and exclaimed: "Chaplain are you hurt?" I excitedly replied, "I haven't time now. Let us take this man away." But almost before I had finished speaking, the terror-stricken surgeon had disappeared and the wounded soldier and I were left alone. At that critical moment a deserter passed along and I caught him by the foot and cried out, "Take hold of this man and help him away from here!" Fortunately the deserter obeyed and we carried the poor man back, I helping as best I could. In a few moments I espied, lying directly in our path, a rebel fuse shell all aglow! It was an awful sight—the thought of stepping over it, like walking into the jaws of death! As we came closer the deserter saw it and tried to get out of the way. If he should turn and run what would become of the wounded man and myself? Before he had time to fully realize the situation I thundered, "Go ahead!" and over the shell with our burden we went. How soon the missile of death exploded we did not remain to investigate. In this battle our brave corps lost heavily. The next morning on Malvern Hill the noble 5th Pennsylvania Reserves mustered only a little over three hundred men! Where were the rest? Wounded and slain! O, the horrors of war!

I did not work long on Tuesday on Malvern Hill. My leg felt sore and I was completely worn out. After the battle had progressed several hours, I lay down with the wounded behind a little hill just in the rear of our ranks, and slept soundly perhaps two hours. I never realized how soldiers could sleep in and during a battle until then.

Next day we came to Harrison's Landing under cover of our gunboats. Here we were safe. I was, by this time, quite sick. As soon as a hospital could be erected, I lay down in charge of Surgeon Lane, and hovered between life and death, until aroused one night early in August by the booming of cannon and the explosion of shells, we were notified to flee for life, as the rebels were on us. I left my cot, went out and saw the shells, like rainbows bursting all around the sky. But the Galena soon got into position and replied, and I crept back again to my bed.

Twice did I, through friends, tender my resignation, and twice was it refused. At length a member of the Christian Commission took my case to Gen. McClellan's headquarters in person, and secured the following general order:

HEADQUARTERS ARMY OF THE POTOMAC,
August 5, 1862. Camp near Harrison's Landing, Va.

Special Order, No. 227.

Leave of absence for twenty days, for the benefit of his health, is granted to Chaplain S. L. M. Conser, 5th Pennsylvania Reserve Corps. At the expiration of that period, should he be unable to rejoin his station, he will proceed as directed by General Order No. 61, of June 7, 1862, from the War Department, Adjutant General's Office.

By command of Maj-Gen., George B. McClellan.

B. WILLIAMS, *A. Adj.-Gen.*

This special order was read at the dress-parade of every regiment of the Army of the Potomac, and I, through the kindness of Surgeon G. Lane, of Chambersburg, was sent home to Baltimore. As Dr. Lane and others were helping me into the ambulance to convey me to the steamer, Maj. Dare put the following note into my hands:

HEADQUARTERS 5TH PENN. RESERVE CORPS.

We take great pleasure in bearing testimony to the correct moral deportment of Rev. S. L. M. Conser, chaplain of this regiment, and we cheerfully commend him to public confidence.

Signed,   J. W. FISHER, *Col.*
GEORGE DARE, *Maj.*

The following was forwarded to me while in the hospital in Baltimore:

To the Honorable Secretary of the Navy:

Sir:—I have pleasure in recommending the Rev. S. L. M. Conser as chaplain in the Navy. He is a pure Christian, an educated gentleman, and a man of talents. He has the entire confidence of his Church.

Signed,   SIMON CAMERON,
Secretary of War.

I most cheerfully and cordially indorse the foregoing.

J. W. FISHER,
Col. 5th Penna. Reserve Corps.

These certificates were very consoling to me, especially Secretary Cameron's recommendation to Secretary Welles, to place me in the navy, but my health was gone, and my age precluded all hopes of recovery. As my resignation had been twice rejected, about March 1, 1863, I asked through our medical purveyor, Simpson, for a court of medical inspection to consider my case. I appeared before the court, and I suppose was pronounced unable to endure the exposure of camp life, for I was at once discharged. And so ended my military career. I did all I could to save my country. I am thankful that my loved flag, though insulted and torn by ungrateful rebels, was born victoriously through the fierce contest, and I do not regret any sacrifice I may have made to keep that banner afloat

"O'er the land of the free and the home of the brave."

www.ingramcontent.com/pod-product-compliance
Lightning Source LLC
Chambersburg PA
CBHW031607110426
42742CB00037B/1320